LOOKING
for an
ANGEL

The Story of Christian Taylor Ferguson

Written by Theda R. Wilson
Illustrated by Kiarra Lynn Smith

If anybody has any information in regards to the case, write to the address below.

Attn: Theda R. Wilson
LOOKING FOR AN ANGEL
P.O. Box 24912
Saint Louis, Missouri 63115

For the memory of Christian Taylor Ferguson
and other missing angels.

For Alonzo Washington and others who fight for
truth, justice and protection

On October 9, 1993 Christian Taylor Ferguson was born. After nine months of waiting, his mother, Theda, was finally able to hold the angel that had been growing inside of her.

Christian's eyes were vibrant brown with long eyelashes. His head was crowned with beautiful, dark curls. Everyone was so excited when they came to visit him in the hospital.

But nobody was happier than Theda.

Christian was born with a rare medical disorder called citrullinemia. This meant that his body was unable to break down proteins found in foods. There was also a chance that nitrogen waste could build up in his bloodstream, creating dangerous levels of ammonia. As a result, Christian was put on a special low-protein diet, taking medication for his survival.

If he did not take his medication, Christian could become seriously ill and suffer from brain damage or even death. Therefore, it was very important that Christian was in good health.

Everyone could tell when Christian was feeling better because he would be boisterous and ready for action! He had a natural talent for bringing joy to the people that surrounded him.

He was always filled with laughter and loved to listen to imaginative stories. Often, he would play in the radiant sunshine. Christian's spirit was as brilliant as a beautiful rainbow.

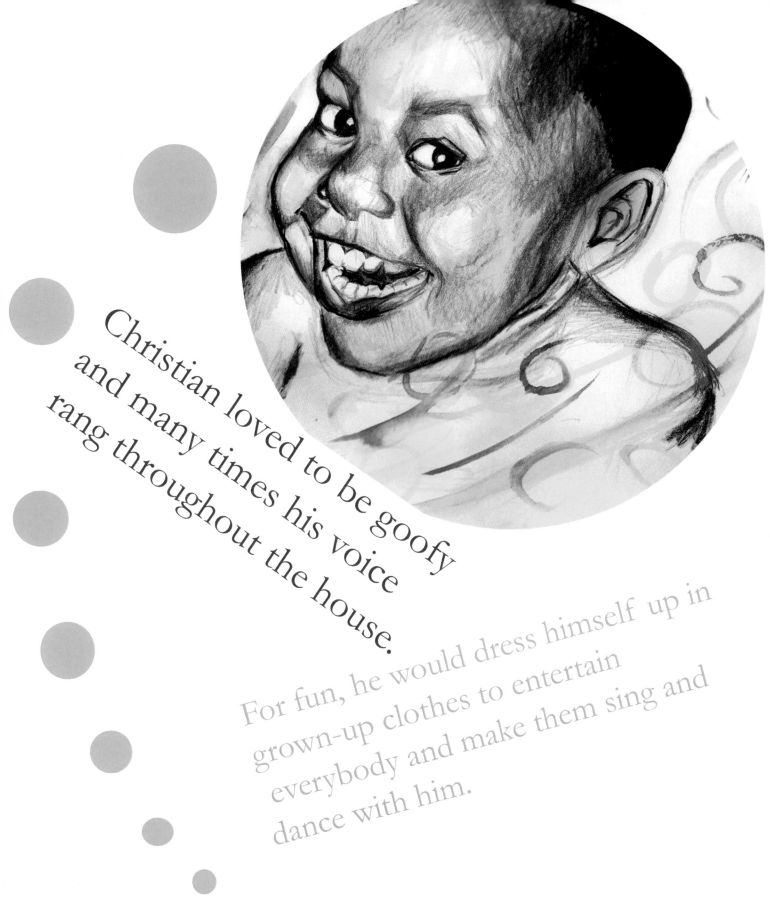

Christian loved to be goofy and many times his voice rang throughout the house.

For fun, he would dress himself up in grown-up clothes to entertain everybody and make them sing and dance with him.

Every moment around Christian was a happy moment.

Christian had a younger brother named Connor. His brother was his best friend and was always at his side.

They spent their days doing many exciting activities such as reading books, playing video games, dancing and running. Christian and Connor had lots of cheerful times together.

Struggling with citrullinemia did not rob Christian of his phenomenal spirit. He still loved everyone and his mother took excellent care of him. He wanted to have a fulfilling life just as every human being wishes to have.

Though Christian's life was an abundance of wonder, it was interrupted by a bitter transformation.

January 16, 2001 was a tragic day for Christian. While he was with his biological father, Christian fell into a coma.

Though it was feared that he would not survive the trauma, miraculously, he pulled through and lived.

However, he became disabled. Christian had to learn to speak and walk all over again. He was the same person, but he had to face the challenges of living in a different body.

Christian continued to be a glad child, despite his circumstances. Though Christian had both physically and mentally changed, this did not stop his mother's love for him. She still hugged him, kissed him and made sure that he was being taken care of, just as she always had.

Theda did not know that Christian's life was about to be altered once again.

On June 11, 2003 Christian was reported missing from Saint Louis, Missouri while in the care of his biological father.

During the early morning hours, Christian's father told police that someone had stolen his vehicle while using a pay phone. Hours later, the vehicle was found, but Christian was not inside.

Many people were heartbroken and began searching for Christian. They formed search teams and looked all over town for the missing boy. His face appeared on the screens of televisions, newspapers and benches. People were very saddened and Christian was always in their thoughts. All waited for a positive outcome of his case.

To make sure that her son would never be forgotten, Theda began the Christian T. Ferguson Memorial Parade. Christian's family and many who honored his memory wore t-shirts with his smiling face on it. The parade was always held in June, the month Christian vanished.

People came to show support and to seek justice for Christian.

Days have become years, but nobody has forgotten about Christian. They will always remember the happiness and vibrancy that he brought to those around him.

We are still waiting for our angel to be found.

CHRISTIAN TAYLOR FERGUSON

On June 11, 2003, at approximately 6:09 A.M., a disabled 9-year-old child named Christian Taylor Ferguson was reported missing from St. Louis, Missouri.

Christian's biological father told police that he was using a pay phone when someone drove away in his SUV. Christian was said to be ill and lying in the vehicle when this crime took place. His father was taken to the police station for further questioning about Christian's disappearance, but he refused to cooperate with law enforcement. Hours later, the SUV was recovered, but the whereabouts of Christian remain unknown.

The 2009 Christian T. Ferguson Parade. Photo by Bill Beene.

Kiarra Lynn Smith shows her missing children's poster.
Photo by Bill Beene.

CHRISTIAN TAYLOR FERGUSON

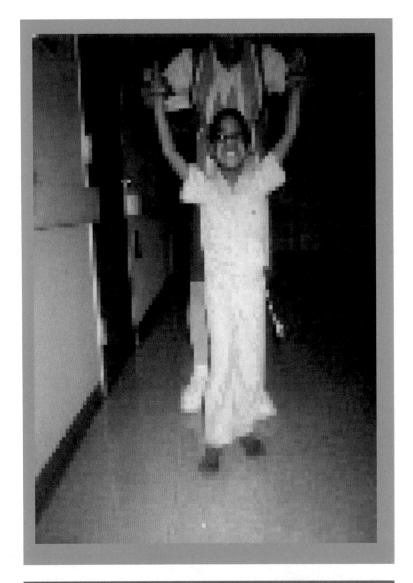

Christian learning how to walk again.

Christian and Heaven.

Christian and Connor playing.   Christian having fun!

Biking for an Angel (2011).

Paula Cosey, mother of missing child, Shemika Cosey (missing since December 2008.)

Dominique singing a song.

Missing posters for a matching game.

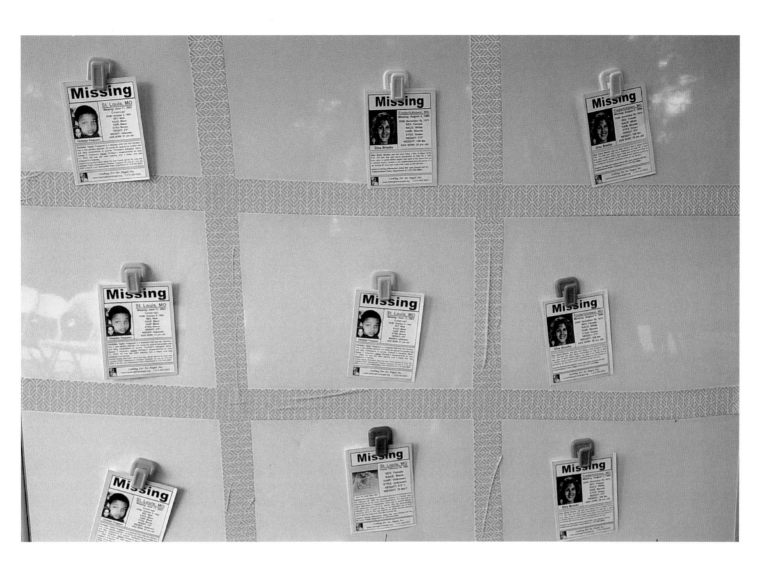

Children's activities: coloring table and matching game.

The band playing at the 2015 Looking for An Angel Event in June.

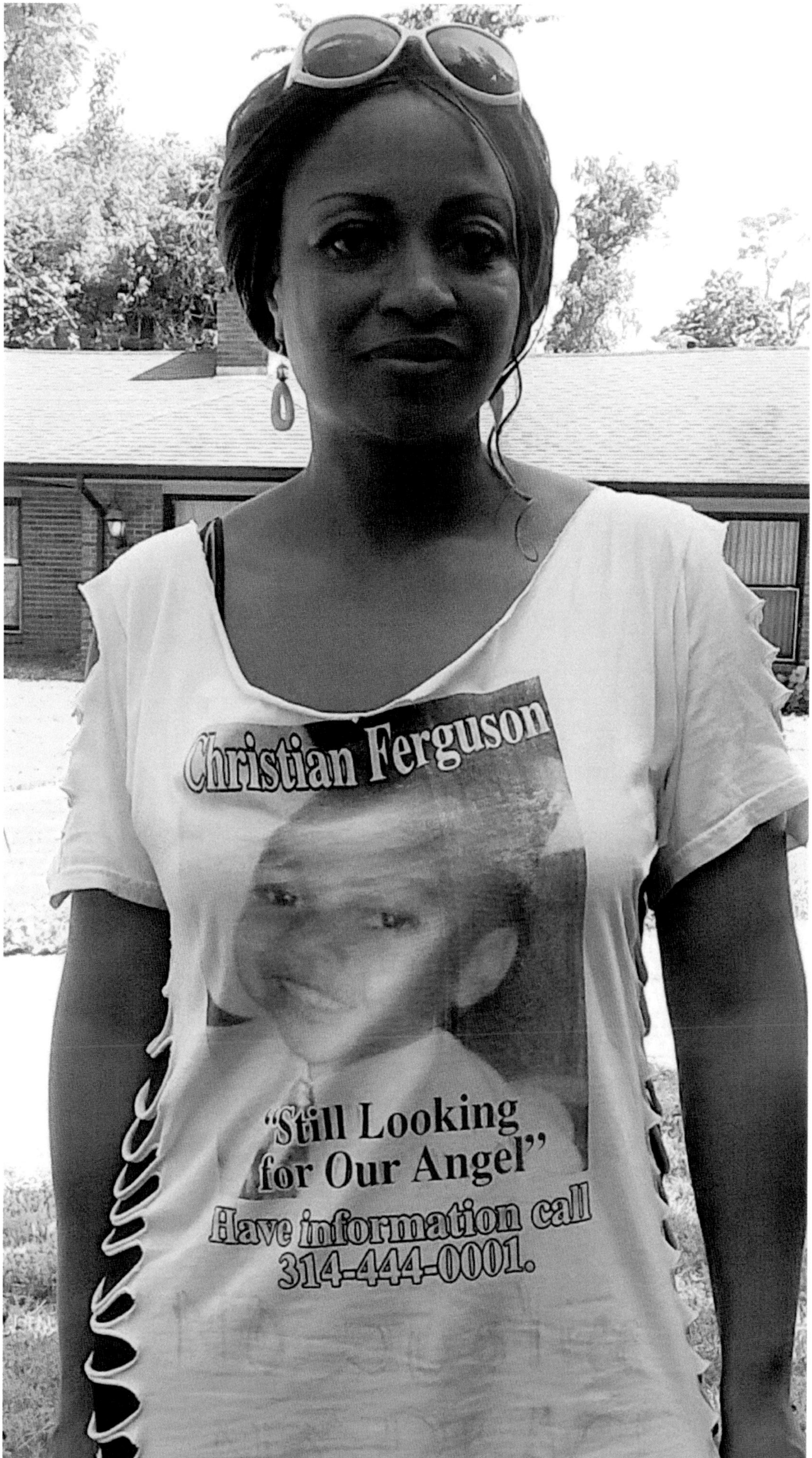
Christian Ferguson
"Still Looking
for Our Angel"
Have information call
314-444-0001.

IMPORTANT THINGS TO REMEMBER (FOR CHILDREN)

1. Always let a trusted adult know where you are.

2. **DO NOT** talk to strangers!

3. **DO NOT** take gifts from strangers.

4. If someone harms or threatens you, tell a trusted adult immediately.

5. **DO NOT** answer the door if you are home alone.

6. Never tell a caller on the phone that you are home alone unless they are trustworthy.

7. If you think someone is being abused or is in danger, tell a trusted adult.

8. **DO NOT BE AFRAID TO SAY "NO!"**

9. Cause a scene and scream for help if you are in danger.

10. In the case of an emergency, call 911!

11. Be careful online. Do not share information or agree to meet someone that you have never met. Do not give out your address, phone number, photographs, birthday, school, church or any other information. BE SAFE WHILE ONLINE!

IMPORTANT THINGS TO REMEMBER
(FOR ADULTS)

1. Talk to your youth about strangers, safety and the potential dangers of people that they do not know or that they think they know.

2. Do not put your child's name on clothing items, bags or anything that can be seen by a stranger. Do not say your child's name aloud around a group of strangers either.

3. Have your child fingerprinted and keep medical information about them in a secure space.

4. Talk to your child often and make sure that he or she is safe whenever you are not around.

5. Know the character of the adults that you leave your child with.

6. Give your child a whistle to wear so that he or she may blow it if in danger.

7. Enroll youth in a self-defense class.

8. Make sure that your home is safe and secure periodically throughout the day.

9. Monitor your child's online activity.

Theda R. Wilson is a woman in search of justice for her family. She is the mother of Christian Ferguson and is the founder of Looking for an Angel, an organization that increases awareness of missing persons and raises monetary awards. She resides in St. Louis, Missouri.

Kiarra Lynn Smith is a visual and literary artist from St. Louis, Missouri. She is the author and illustrator of two books: *Collective Face: a Series of Quatrains on Community Building* and *Let's Speak! Kiswahili: 3 Short Stories Teaching Basic Kiswahili Words.* Smith has a BA in English and Visual Art from Culver-Stockton College.

Made in the USA
Columbia, SC
07 September 2020